The Children's Book of Flowers

A GREEN FIG BOOK

NARCISSUS

The Poet Abu Nuwas (756-814 H.) said describing Narcissus flowers,

تأمل في نبات الأرض وانظر
إلى آثار ما صنع المليك

عيون من لجين شاخصات
بأحداق هي الذهب السبيك

على كثب الزبرجد شاهدات
بأن الله ليس له شريك

Which means,

Contemplate, in the garden of the earth
Behold the traces of God's Creation

Eyes of silver, gazing
with molten golden irises

On peridot stems
Testifying that God has no partners

NAME: ....

Publisher: Green Fig
Pennsylvania, USA
www.gogreenfig.com

Note to Parents & Educators

Beautifully illustrated with simple vocabulary, **The Children's Book of Flowers** by Green Fig peaks the child's interest in the world around him and reinforces his understanding that the universe is made up of bodies and their attributes and that God, the Creator of the universe, does not resemble any of His creations—God's attributes are not like the attributes of His creations. We chose flowers to exemplify a body since children frequently see flowers around them and are able to relate easily to a flower's different attributes.

The Children's Book of Flowers encourages children to ponder about nature and God's creations- an important matter since this increases their faith in God and strengthens their understanding of Tawheed because as the great scholar al-Junayd said, "Tawheed is to differentiate the Creator from the creation." Children will also gain some information about flowers in the process and will enjoy doing the activities provided at the end of the book.

We hope that you will enjoy reading this book with your children over and over again. We would be glad to hear from you at info@gogreenfig.com.

Green Fig Staff

GOD CREATED THE ENTIRE WORLD:

THE UPPER AND THE LOWER AND WHAT IS IN THEM AND IN-BETWEEN THEM.

WE CALL ALL THIS WORLD "THE UNIVERSE".

MOUNTAINS AND TREES...

RIVERS AND SEAS...

SKIES AND STARS...

BUILDINGS AND CARS...

PEOPLE AND ANIMALS...

ALL OF THESE ARE PART OF THE UNIVERSE.
ALL OF THESE ARE BODIES.

ALL BODIES HAVE ATTRIBUTES.

AN ATTRIBUTE OF A BODY IS SOMETHING THAT YOU CAN SEE, HEAR, FEEL, TOUCH, OR SMELL.
ATTRIBUTES DESCRIBE "HOW" A BODY IS.

A FLOWER IS A BODY.
A FLOWER HAS ATTRIBUTES.

Sunflower

A flower has a

Size is an attribute of a body.

Round

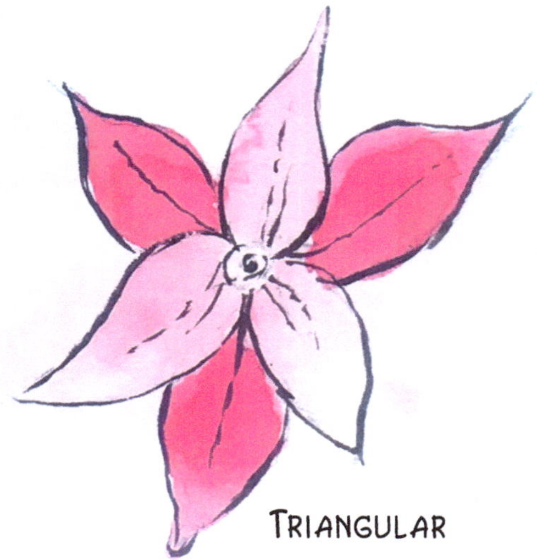

Triangular

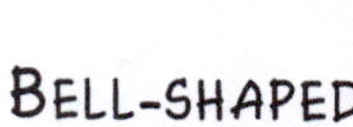

Bell-shaped

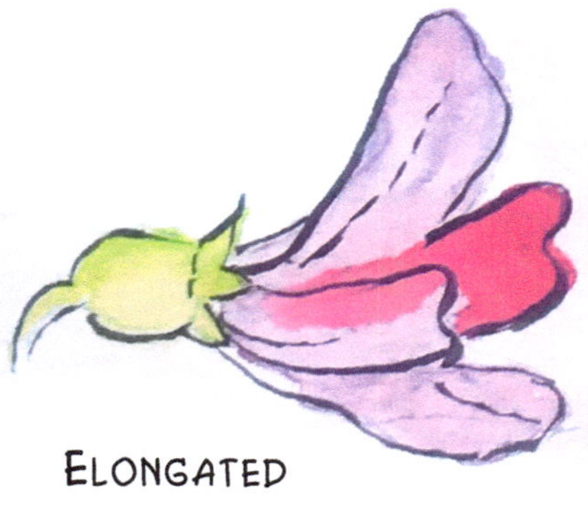

Elongated

A flower has a

shape

Shape is an attribute of a body.

TULIPS

A flower has a

color

Color is an attribute of a body.

A flower has a

smell

Smell is an attribute of a body.

Some flowers feel like velvet

A flower has a

texture

Texture, how something feels,
is an attribute of a body.

JASMINE IN A GARDEN

A flower has a

place

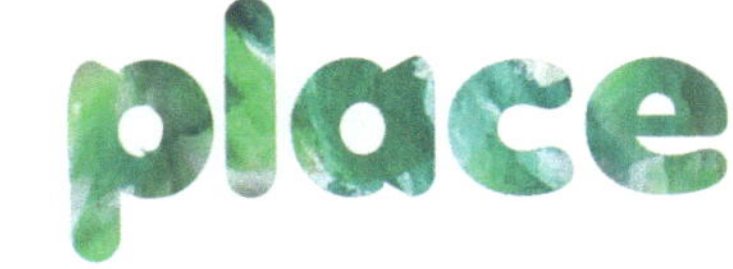

Place is an attribute of a body.

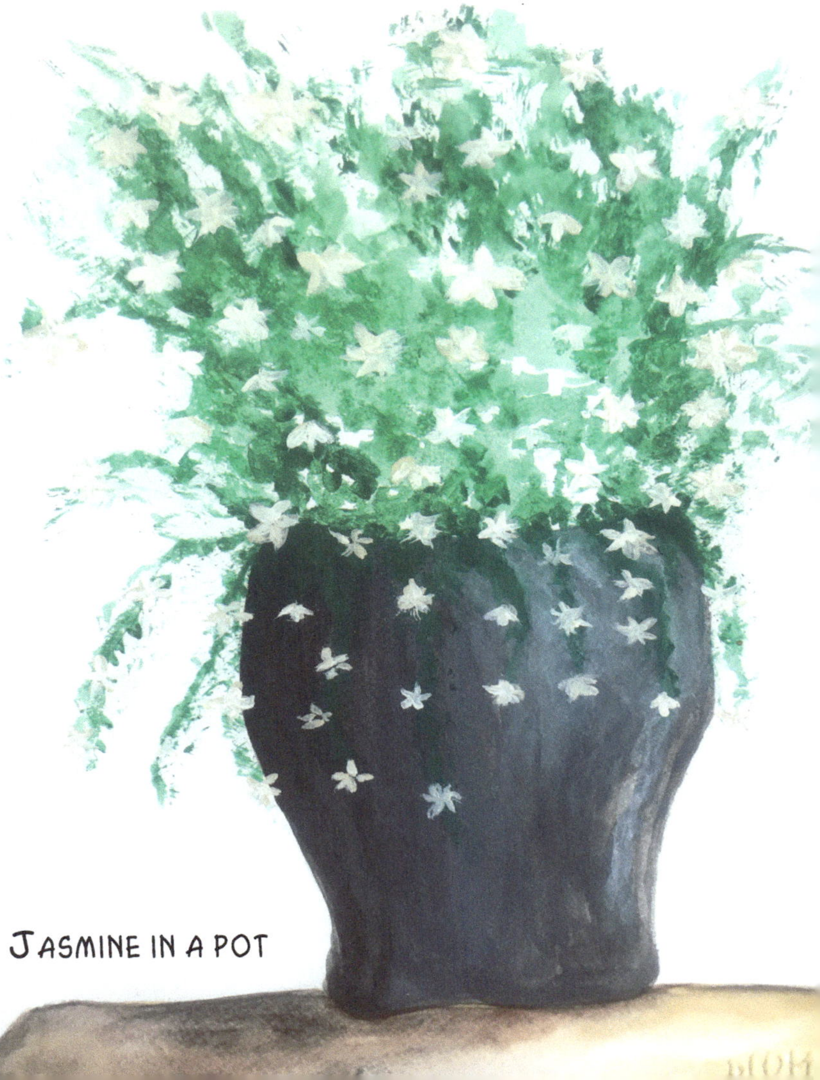

JASMINE IN A POT

Close
Far

A flower is

close or far

from other bodies

Being close or far is an attribute of a body.

Dandelion seedhead

A flower is

still or in motion

Being still or in motion is an attribute of a body.

BuzzZ
Honeysuckle

A flower attracts bees that make a buzzing

sound

Sound is an attribute of a body

A flower

needs

water

Need is an attribute of a body.

petal
anther
filament
sepal
leaf
Stem
roots

A flower is

composed of parts

Being composed of parts is an attribute of a body.

DAFFODILS

A flower

changes

Change is an attribute of a body.

GOD CREATED
"HOW" EACH BODY IS.

GOD IS THE CREATOR OF EACH BODY AND ITS ATTRIBUTES.
GOD IS THE CREATOR OF EVERYTHING.

ACTIVITIES

HOW DO FLOWERS MAKE A GARDENER FEEL?
HAPPY
SAD
ANGRY

ACTIVITIES
WRITE
AN ATTRIBUTE
OF A FLOWER
INSIDE EACH
PETAL.

GLUE HERE OR DRAW YOUR FAVORITE FLOWER

MORE FRAGRANT FLOWERS

MATCH THE NAME OF EACH NICE SMELLING FLOWER TO ITS PICTURE:

TUBEROSE ----------	GARDENIA ----------
CARNATION ----------	JASMINE ----------
LAVENDER ----------	PLUMERIA ----------

2

3

6

5

4

Tuberose 6 - Gardenia 3 - Carnation 4 - Jasmine 1 - Lavender 5 - Plumeria 2

ONE MORE ATTRIBUTE

TASTE IS ANOTHER ATTRIBUTE OF A FLOWER.
DID YOU KNOW THAT ALL PARTS OF A DANDELION CAN BE EATEN?

HOW DO DANDELION'S LEAVES TASTE?

----------- *SWEET*

----------- *BITTER*

----------- *SOUR*

----------- *SALTY*

Bitter

MORE FLOWER SHAPES.

HOW DO THEY LOOK?
MATCH THE SHAPE OF EACH ORCHID TO WHAT IT LOOKS LIKE:

1- *DRACULA SIMIA*
Monkey face

2- *PHALAENOPSIS*
Moth or tiger face

3- *OPHRYS BOMYBLIFLORA*
Laughing bumble bee

4- *ANGULOA UNIFLORA*
Swaddled babies

From right to left: 2 - 4 - 1 - 3

Encourage your child to memorize:

God said in Surat An-Nahl, verse # 60:

Which means:

God has attributes that are not similar to the attributes of others.

The Proud Muslim Kids series by Green Fig is designed to engagingly teach youngsters basic concepts of Islam in a way that speaks to their hearts and minds. Each book in the series is crafted by a staff of qualified educators, writers, illustrators, parents and children. Not only is the Proud Muslim Kids series designed to supplement the early childhood and elementary Islamic curriculum, it is a great addition to any school or home library. Covering a wide variety of topics such as the Five Pillars of Islam, Islamic culture, and Islamic history, parents and children will return to these books and enjoy them together time and time again.

www.ingramcontent.com/pod-product-compliance
Lightning Source LLC
LaVergne TN
LVHW070156110826
845147LV00002B/414

* 9 7 8 1 9 5 3 8 3 6 1 3 7 *